BE A DOG'S BEST FRIEND
A Safety Guide for Kids

*

by Renee Payne, CPDT and Jennifer Gladysz
Illustration by Keith Gladysz

Doggie Couch Books
Brooklyn NY
Copyright © 2009
All Rights Reserved

Special thanks to Raul, Wray and Jake

TABLE OF CONTENTS

Introduction (for adult readers)

The fantasy that dogs and children naturally go together is just that, a fantasy. While it is true that most children love dogs, not all dogs love children. Even well-socialized, kid-proofed dogs have their limitations and their boundaries. It IS important for dog owners to teach their dogs to tolerate children; but ultimately, it's up to parents to properly dog-proof their kids.

According to the National Center for Injury Prevention and Control, close to five million people are bitten by dogs every year. Eight-hundred thousand of those bitten seek medical attention, over half of which are children, most of whom are five to nine years of age. Usually, these bites are to the face, head and neck area.

Our goal is to give parents, teachers and dog trainers a tool to help children learn how to safely interact with dogs, both their own family pets and unfamiliar dogs they may encounter.

Be A Dog's Best Friend features very clear illustrations of dogs demonstrating inviting and uninviting body language, as well as demonstrations of do's and don'ts for children.

The language we've used is geared toward children ages six to ten. For children younger than six, adults can use the text and pictures to begin a dialogue. Ema is our ten-year-old demonstrator. (We worked with dogs we knew would not react dangerously to the "don'ts," and all of Ema's interactions were closely supervised).

If you and your children come away from this book with one lesson, it should be that every dog is an individual and must be assessed as such. Not all Golden Retrievers are friendly, not every Chihuahua will bite, and small dogs aren't necessarily any safer with kids than bigger ones. We hope that with our help, your child will develop the skills to react safely to ALL dogs.

Thank you!

Hi there. I'm Ema.

I'm ten years old and I love dogs!

My mom has her own dog walking service and our friend Renee is a dog trainer, so I'm very lucky; I get to meet lots of dogs!

Do you ever wish you could be like Dr. Doolittle and actually be able to talk to animals? I know I do. Too bad that can't happen, but I have learned the trick to understanding dogs; it's all about reading their body language. Also, we need to understand that every dog is special in their own way.

This book will help you learn safe ways to meet new dogs, to show your own dog that you love him or her, and the important things you should never do around any dog.

I have some friends that are afraid of dogs. If you're afraid, this book will teach you a lot about dealing with dogs and keeping safe. Dogs are wonderful buddies and a lot of fun to play with and to take care of.

I hope you like it!

PART ONE: BODY LANGUAGE

Body language is the way we move our body to communicate. Many times we can just look at someone and tell how they are feeling.

Look at the pictures below. Can you tell when I'm feeling happy? Mad? Sad? Suprised?

Because most people use similar types of facial expressions and movements, it's easy for us to read another person's body language.

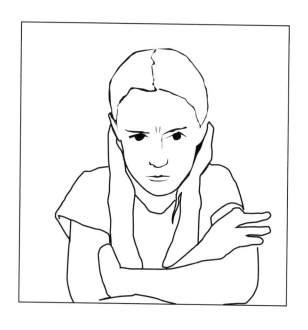 

Dogs use body language too; but because their bodies are different than ours, sometimes it's not as easy to tell how they're feeling.

Many people think that if a dog is wagging his tail he is friendly and happy. Most of the time this is true, but sometimes it isn't.

It's very important to look at more than just a dog's tail.

Let's look at some ways dogs use their other body parts to tell us how they feel.

Stiff Body / Relaxed Body: Look at these two pictures of the same dog.

In which picture does the dog look relaxed?

Can you see where she looks stiff?

When would it be a better idea to approach this dog?

 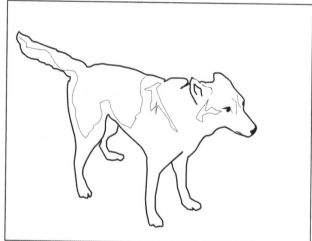

Cowering and Tail Tucking:

If a dog is cowering, he is trying to make himself small -- that means he's scared! And sometimes when dogs are scared they bite.

So when you see a dog that has his tail under his body and he's low to the ground, he's asking you to please go away. You should always respect a dog's wishes and leave him alone.

Sometimes if you go sit down quietly this will help a scared dog understand that you are nice. If you wait, he may come up to sniff you. Go slow and don't make any fast movements. Wait for his signal that it's ok to pet him and have his owner nearby to help you make friends.

Growling and Showing Teeth: This is an easy one! It is never a friendly sign when a dog is growling and showing teeth at a person. Stay away from him!

Sometimes growling can be "talking" for a dog, like when he's playing with a toy or with another dog.

My dog Bowie growls when she wants to play or to go outside. She also makes that noise when I ask her to do something and she's "talking back" to me! This is ok, because I know Bowie very well and my mom explained what this growling means.

If a dog growls and you don't know what he's trying to say, make sure an adult knows and they will help you to understand if he's just talking or if he's warning you to stay away. It's always better to play it safe!

Play Bow:

Can you see what this dog is doing now? This is called a play bow and it's a dog's way of inviting you or another dog to play.

Rolling Over and Showing Belly:

This is a good one! If a dog rolls over onto his back
and shows you his belly, he wants to be friends. That's his way of saying, "scratch right here!"

Barking: Dogs bark for many reasons. They could be saying hello or asking you to play; or they could be afraid of you or warning you to stay away. If a dog you don't know is barking at you, play it safe and don't approach him.

PART TWO: HOW TO SHOW A DOG YOU LOVE HIM

Think about the people who love you. How can you tell? Is it from hugs and kisses? Or maybe the special times you spend together? Is it the way they take care of you? Or the games you play with each other? There are many ways to show love.

When it comes to showing a dog you love him, you might need to think about what HE likes more than what you like. We need to remember that not every dog likes all the ways people use to show love. Let your dog tell you what's ok and respect his space, mood and wishes.

Some dogs love hugs and petting.

Some dogs love to play ball.

Some dogs love when you sit by them and watch TV.

Some dogs love to go with you to training class.

Remember: No dog likes to have his tail pulled. Also, never tease a dog, especially with food or a toy.

Most dogs don't love to be picked up but if an adult says it's ok, here's how: Place one arm around the dog's chest and your other arm should cradle his behind.

Feeding Your Dog: If an adult says it's ok, it can be your job to feed your dog every day. This is a great way to help take care of your dog, but remember, never walk up to your dog's food WHILE he's eating.

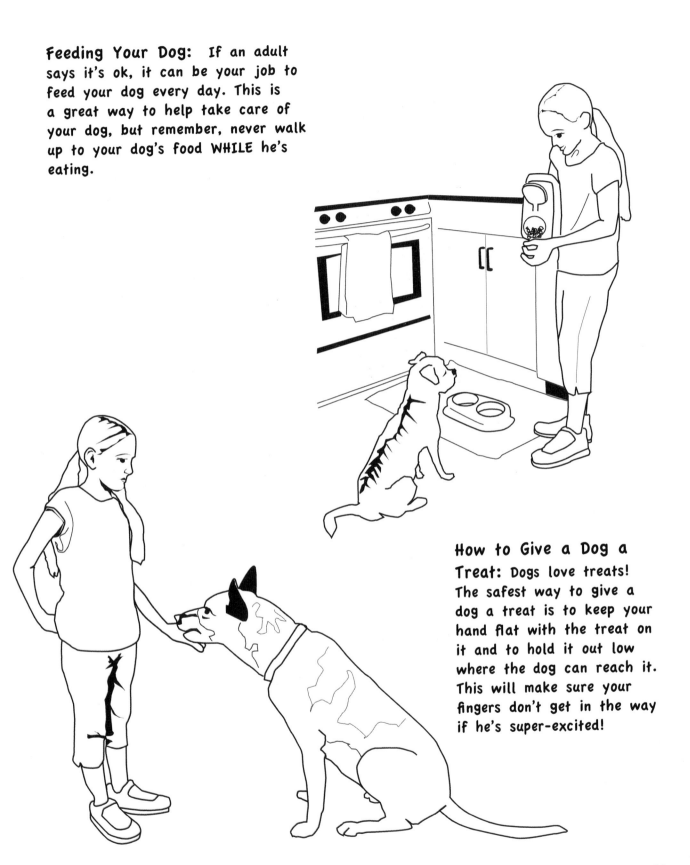

How to Give a Dog a Treat: Dogs love treats! The safest way to give a dog a treat is to keep your hand flat with the treat on it and to hold it out low where the dog can reach it. This will make sure your fingers don't get in the way if he's super-excited!

Your Dog's Crate: Some dogs have a crate that they like to hang out and sleep in. This is their bedroom. It's never ok to crawl into your dog's crate - whether he's in it or not. Help make your dog's crate nice for him with blankets, toys and treats if your parents say it's ok.

Playing with Your Dog: Playing with your dog is fun! Maybe your dog likes to play fetch, run with you at the park or play with his toys.

Just be careful not to make your dog too excited. When this happens he might hurt you by mistake. It's good to take breaks while you're playing together.

Also be careful when playing tug of war; this might be a game left for the adults.

12

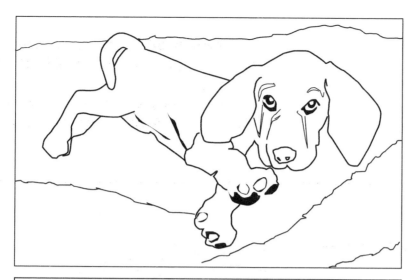

Young Puppies: If you have a young puppy, be extra careful not to get him too excited. Puppies like to nip when they play with other puppies their age. When they get too excited, they might play with you this way. Your puppy is just playing, but those teeth are very sharp! If your puppy likes to use his mouth a lot, give him a toy to chew on instead.

PART THREE: WHAT TO DO WHEN...

What to do when your dog gets mad:

Just like people get mad, dogs can get mad or upset too. Maybe you've gotten too close to their bone or favorite toy or maybe they don't feel like being pet or played with right now. Dogs show that they're mad by getting stiff, growling, or showing teeth.

GGRRRR....

If this happens, just back away quietly. Don't run, scream or point. And never hit! Tell an adult right away. The good news is, dogs don't stay mad! They usually forget all about it once you back off and leave them alone.

What to do when your dog's been bad:
Sometimes dogs do things that make us mad, like peeing in the house or ripping up our favorite toys. If your dog does do something bad, never yell, point or scold him. And never hit. Go tell an adult.

Important:
Dogs don't know the difference between their own toys and your toys. Your toys might even seem better to your dog, since they smell like you and you're their best buddy.

So remember, don't leave your toys where your dog can get them.

If you have a mad or bad dog, it may be time for some training. Talk to an adult to see if you can take your dog to class or have a trainer come over to the house to help him learn to behave. It can be a lot of fun for you and your dog to learn new things together.

PART FOUR: MEETING NEW DOGS

I love to meet new dogs! But there are some things to remember when you're meeting a dog for the first time.

The most important thing is to ask the dog's owner if it's ok to say hello. If the owner says yes, then here's what you want to keep in mind – we'll start with what you should do and then I'll tell you some things you should NOT do.

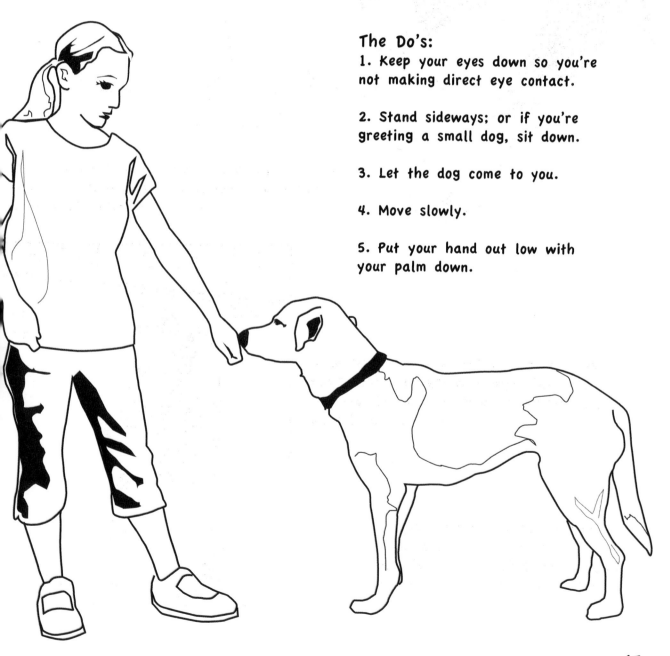

The Do's:
1. Keep your eyes down so you're not making direct eye contact.

2. Stand sideways; or if you're greeting a small dog, sit down.

3. Let the dog come to you.

4. Move slowly.

5. Put your hand out low with your palm down.

Most Important: Let the dog decide if he wants you to pet him. He'll let you know by showing you friendly body language such as having a relaxed body, wagging his tail and moving closer to you. There's nothing better than a happy, friendly dog!

And now the fun part! When it's time to pet the dog, pet his back, sides and under his chin. Pet him with long, slow strokes.

Caution: If the dog seems uninterested in you, leave him alone! This may be a sign he doesn't want to be your friend, and he could turn unfriendly if you try to get close to him.

The Don'ts:

1. Never bother a sleeping dog. I know I hate to be woken up, too!

2. Don't stare into a dog's face. In dog language, staring into another dog's face can be a sign of anger or bossiness.

3. Never pet a dog that is behind a fence. Sometimes dogs get mad when they feel trapped. It's kind of like not bothering the animals at the zoo!

4. Don't pat a dog on the head. Some dogs don't like that. They usually prefer strokes, almost like you're brushing them with your hands.

5. Never approach a dog if he has food or a toy. Dogs don't always know how to share.

6. Never approach a dog that is tied up outside of a store or in a yard – even if they look cute and friendly!

7. Don't stand over or lean over a dog, especially a small dog. You might scare them.

8. Never pick up a small dog. It's rude!

9. If a dog offers kisses, that's great... but never put your face next to a dog's mouth to ask for them.

What to do when a strange dog comes up to you and the owner is not around: This can be a little scary, and when you're scared or nervous it's easy to do the wrong things... so remember, don't stare, scream or run. Never raise your arms and make jerky movements. Just wait quietly with your head down until the dog goes away. Then slowly back away (don't run) and tell an adult.

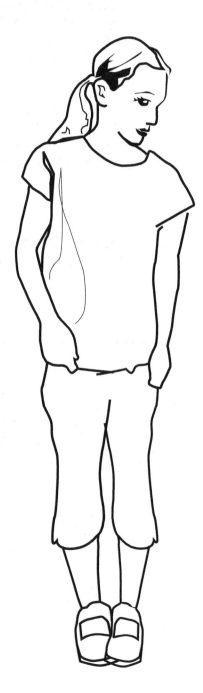

PART FIVE: DOG RUN / DOG PARK

Dogs need a lot of exercise and playtime with their doggie friends. Going to the dog run can be a fun time. I love taking my dog Bowie to the dog run with my mom. Bowie has a good time playing with her pals, plus I get to meet a bunch of different dogs. It takes a lot of patience, but I always make sure to stay out of the way while the dogs are playing. They usually come and say hello to me during a break from the action!

Just remember, a dog run is not like a regular park and there are special rules we must follow.

Lots of dog parks have a big sign with the rules on them – rules for both the dogs AND the people. If your dog park doesn't have a sign, here are some things that you'll want to keep in mind.

Never bring people food into the dog run. I learned that the hard way when Bowie's friend Jimmy stole my sandwich!

As fun as it is, never give out dog treats (even though there might be people in the run that do). Many dogs will fight over treats.

Leave the toys at home! Sometimes you'll see people at the run with toys and balls for the dogs, but this really isn't a safe thing to do. Some dogs will fight over toys or balls. Never raise your arms, run or scream. Dogs think you're inviting them to jump up on you.

Don't pick up small dogs, even if they look like they want to be picked up. You might think you're protecting them but they become bait for the other dogs. Also, if they're sitting in your lap, they might try to guard you from other dogs.

Watch out for running dogs; they might knock you over by accident. Sit quietly on the bench or stand near the grown-ups.

The dog run is not really a place for small children.

Oh no, Jimmy wants my lunch!

Toys are not safe in the run... even though Jimmy and Bowie are good friends, they might fight over the ball!

It's fun and safe to sit quietly and watch the pups playing!

Dog Play: A trip to the dog run is a time for your dog to play with his friends. It's a lot of fun to watch but sometimes it can look scary to us if we don't understand what dog play looks like.

Many of the things that dogs are not supposed to do with humans, they CAN do when they're playing with other dogs. It's normal for dogs to show teeth to their dog friends.

Dogs climb on each other, play fight, growl and bark. This is all normal dog fun for them.

Sometimes dogs do get into real fights. These fights usually look and sound a lot scarier than they really are. But if this happens, don't scream. Just stay out of the way. The adults will take care of it.

Conclusion (for kids)

Dogs can be lots of fun! Just be careful, read their body language and respect their wishes. Listen to your parents and dog owners to stay safe.

And remember, if you're still afraid of dogs, it's ok. Maybe you can find someone with a sweet dog that you can slowly get used to being around. If you have friends that are afraid of YOUR dog, try to make them more comfortable. And be sure not to tease them!

Have a good time playing with and taking care of the dogs in your life!

Conclusion (for adults):

Having a dog teaches our children responsibility and can provide them with a loyal companion. Before you bring a dog into your home, just keep in mind that a safe family pet takes work, and it's up to you to kid-proof your dog.

It's easy to fall in love with that puppy in the window, but spontaneous puppy purchases can quickly prove to be a big mistake.

When it's time to pick out the family dog, do your research first. Find a reputable trainer and vet in your area and speak with them before even getting a dog. The more information you have, the better informed your choice will be.

You'll need to consider your family's schedule, level of activity, and the age of your children. The decision should also be made as to whether a puppy or older dog would be most appropriate for your household.

Whether you decide on a mixed breed or purebred, remember that about 4 million dogs* pass through United States shelters each year. Many of these dogs would make wonderful family pets.

Mixed breeds tend to have considerably fewer genetic health issues than purebreds; but if you do have your heart set on a purebred, 25-30% of dogs in shelters are purebreds.* If you can't find the specific breed that you want at your local shelter, breed rescue groups have access to dogs of all ages and temperaments. But keep in mind that evaluating a dog's temperament is much more important than looking for a specific breed.

If you do decide to purchase a dog, never buy one at a pet store. Always work with a reputable breeder. Again, speak to your trainer and vet about this; they can help you find one.

After you bring your new family member home, take a training class and learn how to properly socialize, kid-proof and communicate with your dog.

And remember, socialization, playtime with other dogs, exercise and training are the keys to a well-behaved dog.

*Human Society United States

Resources for kids:

"Raising Puppies & Kids Together: A Guide for Parents" by Pia Silvani

Clicker Puppy DVD by Doggone Crazy

Just for fun:

www.dogster.com
www.mydarndog.com

Resources for Adults:

Culture Clash – Jean Donaldson
Don't Shoot The Dog – Karen Pryor
Clicker Training for Dogs – Karen Pryor
Dogs For Dummies – Gina Spadafori
On Talking Terms With Dogs: Calming Signals – Turid Rugaas

Finding a Trainer:

www.apdt.com

Adoptions:

www.petfinder.com

AKC (breed-specific rescue organizations):

www.akc.org/rescue/cfm

Index of doggie pictures:

Renee Payne, CPDT owns Walk This Way Canine Behavior Therapy in New York City, and has been training dogs and their humans since the mid-1990's. Renee graduated from the Animal Behavior Center of New York, is a Certified Pet Dog Trainer and specializes in canine behavior problems. She has been interviewed by CBS News, Fox News, CNN, The New York Times, Esquire magazine and various other media outlets as a behavior expert. Renee also contributes articles on dog training and behavior to numerous magazine and websites.

Jennifer Gladysz is a trained dog handler and the owner of Mobile Mutts Dog Walking and Cat Sitting in Brooklyn, NY. She has been a dog owner most of her life and has been walking dogs since 2003. She currently has three pups of her own. Jennifer is also a mom with experience teaching kids how to behave around dogs.

Keith Gladysz is married to Jen and co-owner of Mobile Mutts. He received his under-graduate and graduate degrees from NYU, and organized an Art Collective at the Walt Whitman Birthplace with Jen. He's also a musician, artist and designer.

Made in the USA
Lexington, KY
29 May 2013